Ladies and Lipstick

These glamorous ladies depict true leisure. Admiring a blossom or perfecting their make-up, these ladies seem to have not a care in the world. On the little towel, blue lines are accented with pink satin stitch for the fingernails, lips and lipstick tip.

The red linen hankie bears the single word "Lipstick" in script. These special red hankies were designed to blot away excess lipstick. The color red made the lipstick invisible on the red cloth. Collectible lipstick blotter hankies are often decorated with faces of ladies or kissing lips? Just a bit of whimsy?

Hint: Take a tip from the anonymous needlewoman and explore stitching in white on bold colors. There is no rule that says backgrounds have to be white!

see patterns on pages 24 - 25

Create ladies for every occasion with beautiful tinted linens and simple embroidery stitches.

The Image of a Lady

The exquisite detail and flowing lines in this design spell out grace and serenity. A tinted central image and the surrounding border enhance the effect. Everything about the motif, stitched here on ecru linen, is in perfect balance. Embroidery stitches over the tinted fabric create a beautiful rich texture.

Hint: If you're making this for a gift, vary the hair color to match the lucky recipient.

see pattern on pages 26 - 27

Three Modern Misses

No frills and ruffles for these modern gals: They're active and up-to-date - for their era, that is. And they have an attitude of wealth and comfort. Their leisure activities look expensive, perhaps because it was the Depression era and these images were a fantasy of better times to come.

Subtle tinting and bold outline stitching make these classy designs a refreshing breath of fresh air. Choose from the equestrienne, the sailing enthusiast or the motorist, or stitch all three.

Hint: Choose black floss for the outline to achieve the crisp graphic look of the originals.

see patterns on pages 28 - 33

*Ladies enjoy
leisure time activities...
boating, horseback
riding and driving...*

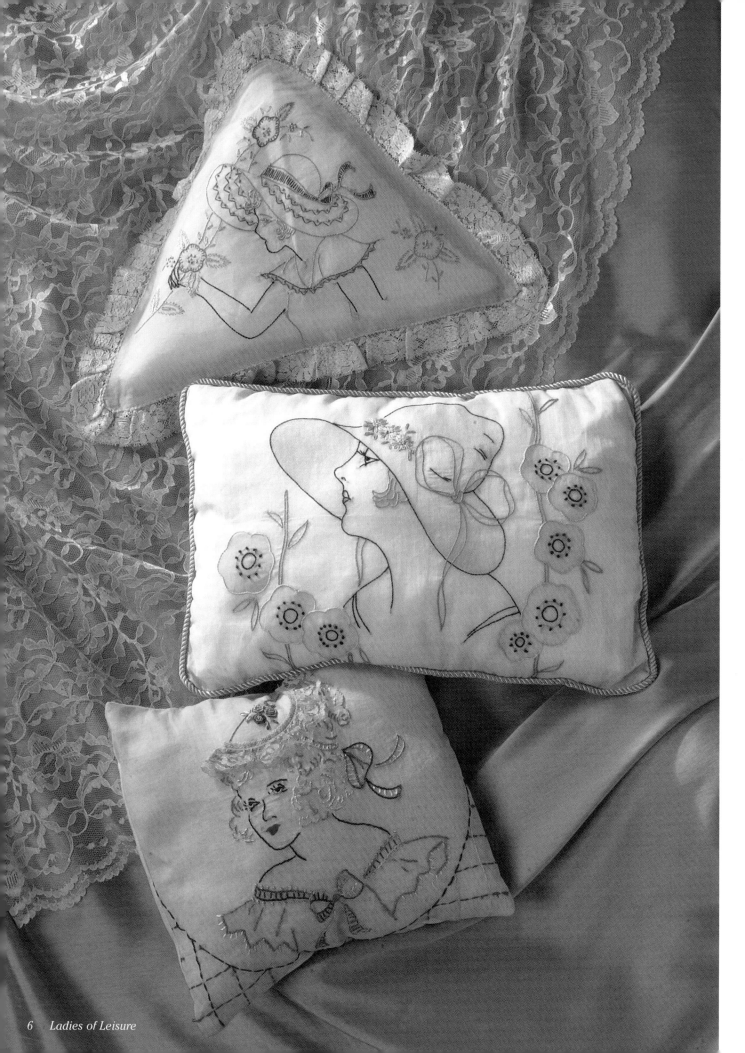

Some of these pillows include rayon threads, which are an unusual addition for the time.

Although women did wear big bonnets and other chic chapeaux, the image is also part of the fantasy of leisure. The motif has certainly become a symbol of the era; well over half the designs in this book feature them.

Notice the ribbon trimming the bonnet at lower right. It's left free, merely held in place by ribbon roses here and there.

Hint: Try crayon tinting on pastel shades of sheer fabric for an even richer look.

see patterns on pages 34 - 41 and 60

Sheer and Sensational

Something special happens when you embroider on organdy or other sheer fabrics. The shadow of the thread as it passes beneath the surface creates another pattern that is quite mysterious—especially black or other dark-colored floss. Add to that effect the look of tinting, and you have a wonderful feast for the eyes.

A Gracious Gathering

Making decorative throw pillows is a great way to utilize worn linens that still include beautiful embroidery. The ones shown here probably began life as pillowcases or table scarves. Although they'd add grace to a bed, don't overlook the "shabby chic" appeal of vintage linens on white wicker furniture. The picture, however, was probably designed for the oval frame.

This gathering likely includes work ranging from the twenties through the forties.

Hint: Don't stop with embroidery. Sort through your stash of trimmings and choose those with a vintage look to add the finishing touch to your creation.

see patterns on pages 42 - 45

Lovely ladies love to garden, walk in the sunshine and visit.

Organized Ladies
shown on page 10

Each day of the week had its own special chore. Baking, laundry, ironing, cleaning. It was a never-ending round. But these energetic ladies carried it off with style. Today we do our tasks whenever we get a chance, but it would still be fun to have a set of these vintage towels.

Choose from the ultra-simple set on page 10 with each lady set in a perfect circle, or the more detailed set shown above the simple set. Note the little touches: music notes coming from the church, the little dog under the table, the bird in the tree.

Some creations from past decades were for "show," but others were meant to be used.

Hint: Stitch a set of kitchen towels for a new bride, and include a note encouraging her to really use them - not set them aside. see patterns on pages 50 - 57

CHURCH ON SUNDAY

SATURDAY BAKE

CLEAN ON FRIDAY

MARKET ON THURSDAY

Petticoats and flouncy skirts were popular every day of the week!

MONDAY

TUESDAY

WEDNESDAY

THURSDAY

FRIDAY

SATURDAY

SUNDAY

Precious petticoats, bonnets and long skirts give vintage nostalgia to these designs.

The Simple Things

If this industrious housewife is intimidated by the giant objects in her life, she shows no trace of it. Linen towels depict - in great detail - a lady at her domestic tasks. Is that Father himself in the portrait on the wall, watching over her as she polishes his special cup?

A contented couple is pictured on this tea towel with a woven border. They're dressed in formal finery, and tiny multicolored French knots form her bouquet. Perhaps they're celebrating an important anniversary. The lack of a veil tells us it is not a wedding portrait.

Hint: Be free in your interpretation of these motifs. Change the colors around, or stitch the design in a single color. Add applique or tinting to any of the patterns.

see patterns on pages 58 - 61

Perky ladies adorn pillowslips.
What a delightful way to fall asleep.

Here are a group of the best designs depicting ladies of leisure. All the accessories are in place - ribbons, flowers, parasols and swirling curves of greenery. Take a tip from the trims of vintage days as well as rickrack, lace, fabric edging and crochet, all of which you can also buy by the yard!

Hint: If you can sew at all, it's easy to make custom pillowcases in any size, fabric and color that strikes your fancy. If you want to emphasize the vintage look, you can age brand-new fabrics by washing them several times in hot water and just a little bleach.

see patterns on pages 63 - 73

Dreams of Leisure

So many things from years gone by are no longer practical for everyday use. We don't want to iron rows of tucks or fasten dozens of buttons. But pillowcases remain a perfect place to show off fine embroidery. And it's so easy to stitch on pillowcases you've purchased.

Potholder
Girl

Vintage Aprons

As we go about our daily tasks, we're probably wearing jeans. But yesterday's ladies popped a pretty apron over their equally pretty dresses. You might hang an apron from a hook as a decorative accent in your kitchen rather than actually putting it on. But it might be fun for a party or family holiday.

The apron at upper left certainly takes the cake! Its colors and style show great design and attention to detail. The vivid yellow of the lady's hair, echoed in the color of the cake, is strong and bright, while the blue of her frock is repeated in the canisters. The rounded pockets look like little bowls. Lace trim and simple embroidery stitches complete the picture. In a more old-fashioned style, the bonneted beauty combines a touch of applique with lattice-like embroidery.

Hint: Take liberties with embroidery stitches. Just because the original used a certain stitch doesn't mean you have to. Use your favorites or take a chance learning something new.

see patterns on pages 74 - 79

These three aprons are prime examples of the way our ancestors combined the images of ladies of leisure with the practical necessity of protecting themselves from the spills encountered during work.

Note: The applique calico skirt on the peach linen apron appears to be three tiers, but the skirt is really cut from one piece of fabric - the rows of running stitches enhance the effect.

On the pink organdy apron, subtle colors and a touch of lace combine for pure femininity.

Check out the exquisite detail on the butterflies and flowers - super easy to stitch but beautiful.

Hint: Variegated floss creates a great look. With the same simple stitches, you can achieve a very rich effect.

see patterns on pages 80 - 85

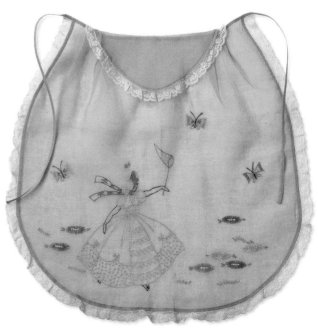

Exotic Ladies

Exotic Lady Bag

Now don't confuse a lady bag with a bag lady. The glamorous creature shown above, center stage, adorns a satin foldover bag that was probably used to hold jewelry or stockings for travel. It's certainly elegant enough for a trip on the Orient Express.

Embroider the top part of the lady and create her bouffant skirt with a tidbit of tulle. The feather fan would look lovely tinted and embroidered.

Tip: Purchased edging completes this vintage example.

see patterns on pages 86 - 87 and 90

Perky Pincushion Dolls

Pin Ladies

Pincushion skirts provide a base for porcelain tops made in Germany in the 1930s. The result is pure boudoir glamour. The taller lady wears blue calico over a net underskirt, while her petite sister is decked out in lace over satin.

Pincushion Dolls

These wide-eyed little girls in their Sunday best would add a touch of whimsy to any sewing room. Cute little cone-shaped hats and a fluffy bonnet give them a finishing touch.

Their two-piece body shape is simple to sew and is amazingly functional.

Porcelain and chalk faces combined with taffeta and moire fabrics make these little dolls elegant. Add silk and satin ribbons to dress them in hats, collars, belts and accessories.

Hint: If you want your "vintage" linens to have an authentic look, consider using bits of old fabrics for appliqué and trim. Don't destroy an item that might be historically valuable, though.

see patterns on pages 88 - 89

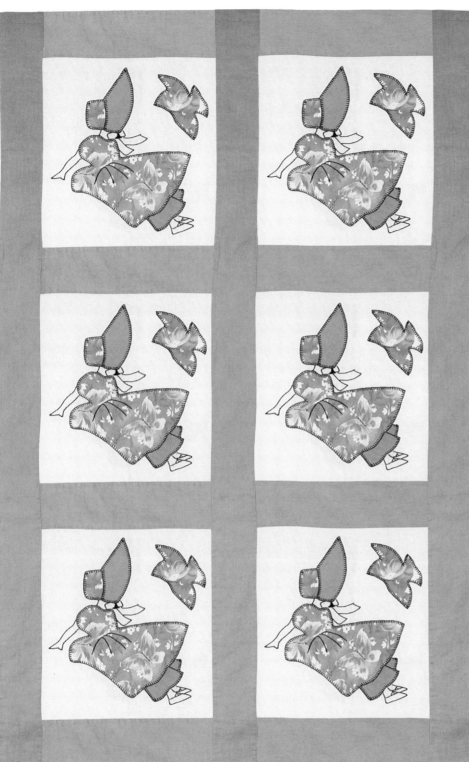

Sitting Pretty... Choose your favorite stitches and fabrics. This would be a perfect quilt for a little girl. You could use bits of her favorite outgrown clothing for the applique to make a priceless personal memento.

Sitting Pretty

Repeat the blocks for a quilt, as shown, or make just one and use it for a pillow. Applique the bird, bonnet, dress and pantaloons, then embroider the rest. Blanket stitch and black floss are used for the applique and embroidery details.

see patterns on pages 19-21

Sitting Pretty Quilt

FINISHED SIZE: $32^1/2$" x 47"
MATERIALS:
- 44" wide, 100% cotton fabrics:
    - A - $1^3/4$ yards White fabric for design blocks
    - B - 3 yards Pink fabric for bonnet brims, pantaloons, sashings, borders, backing and binding
    - C - $1/4$ yard of Pink print fabric for dresses, bonnet backs and butterflies
- 36" x 50" piece of batting
- 3 skeins of DMC embroidery floss 310 Black
- Pink sewing thread

DESIGN BLOCKS:
1. Cut six 12" x 12" squares from A.
2. Transfer one of each of the designs on pages 20 - 21 onto the center of each A square.
3. Make a template for the skirt, bonnet back, bonnet brim, dress, pantaloons and butterfly on pages 20 and 21. If desired, use a glue stick to attach the templates for the bonnet brim and pantaloons to the wrong side of B. Place the right side of the template down.
4. Repeat to attach the templates for the dresses, bonnet backs and butterfly to the back of C.
5. Cut around each template, leaving a $1/4$" seam allowance around all edges. Clip curves.
6. Place each piece right side down on an ironing board. Spray the edges of each piece with heavy-duty spray starch. Fold back the $1/4$" seam allowance around the edges and iron it in place. Ease curves, make corners crisp.
7. Applique the pieces in place.
8. Use 2 strands of floss to embroider along the dashed lines on each design.
9. Use 2 strands of floss to embroider buttonhole stitches around the edges of the appliqued pieces.

SASHING:
1. Use $1/4$" seam allowance throughout.
2. Cut four $3^1/2$" x 12" strips from B.
3. Cut one $3^1/2$" x 41" strip from B.
4. With right sides facing, sew a 12" strip between 2 design blocks.
Repeat with the remaining 12" strips and 4 blocks to make a total of two 3-block rows.
5. Sew the 41" strips between 3 block rows. Sew the other strip below the bottom row.

BORDERS:
1. Cut 2 side borders each $3^1/2$" x 41" from B.
2. Cut two top and bottom borders $3^1/2$" x $32^1/2$" from B.
3. With right sides facing, sew the side borders in place. Trim ends even. Repeat to sew top and bottom borders in place. Trim all edges even.

BACKING:
1. Cut a 44" x 54" piece from A.
2. Layer the backing, batting and the assembled top to form a sandwich. Center the quilt top on the batting. Baste all of the layers together.
3. Quilt the quilt as desired.
4. Remove the basting stitches. Trim the batting even with the edges of the quilt top.

BINDING:
1. Cut $2^1/2$" strips from B for the binding.
2. Refer to the instructions below to attach the binding.

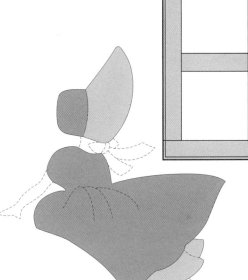

Sitting Pretty Quilt Assembly Diagram

Sew two 12" sashing strips between 3 design blocks to make a row. Make 2 rows.

Binding Instructions

1. Cut the binding strips along the grain of the fabric according to the quilt instructions.
2. Sew enough strips together, end - to - end, to go around the quilt. Press seams open.
3. Fold the strip in half lengthwise, with wrong sides facing.
4. Pin the raw edge of the binding strip to align with the raw edges of the quilt top/batting/backing sandwich.
5. Machine sew the binding strip in place, stitching through all layers.
6. At the corner, leave the needle in place through the fabrics and fold the binding up straight. Fold it up and over into a mitered corner.
7. Fold the folded edge of the binding to the back and whip stitch the edge in place. Miter the corners on the front and on the back. Stitch corners closed.

Fold strip in half, wrong sides facing.

Align all raw edges.

Leave the needle in position at the corner. Fold the binding up and back to miter.

Sitting Pretty Quilt

see photo on page 18

Six little girls, wearing six pretty bonnets meet up with six lovely patterned birds. Said each one to the other, "Oh, I just love your colors and, you're trimmed out very nicely too!"

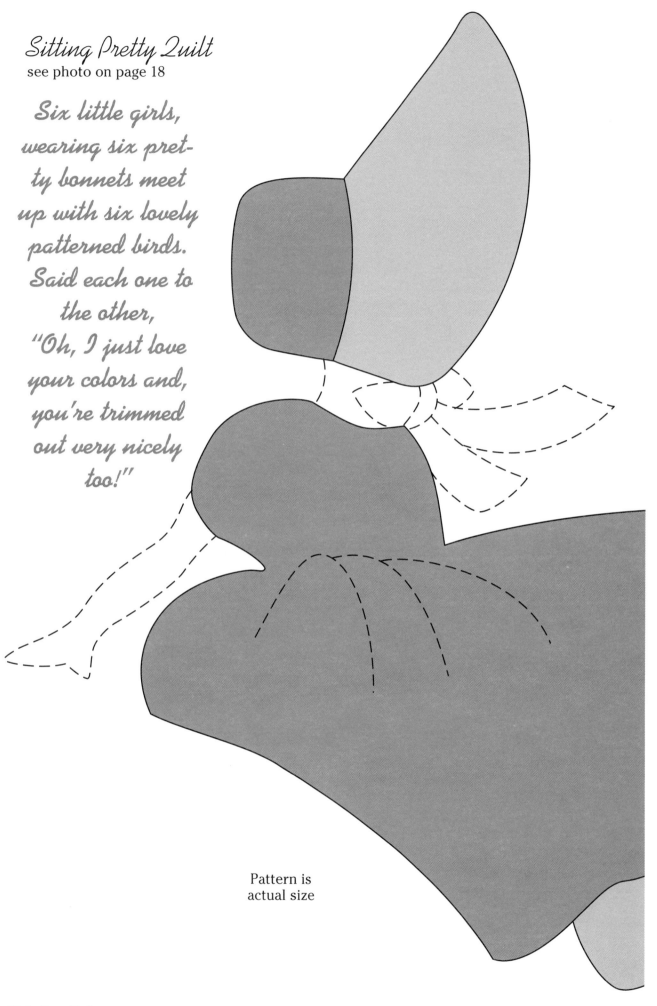

Pattern is actual size

Profile of a Lady
see photo on page 2

Pattern is
actual size

*Lovely flowers in blue and red
How brilliant your colors.
Your smell is sweet as tho
kissed by the dew.
From your pot to my bonnet
you'll make the transition and
ride about town in fashionable style.*

Enlarge pattern 110%
to measure about
6" wide.

Ladies and Lipstick
see photo on page 3

Pattern is
actual size

*A rose by any other
name should smell
so sweet.*

Patterns are
actual size

*A woman's just not dressed unless
she has her lipstick on!*

Lipstick

*I met her when I was a boy, we were school mates.
I guess what I remember most about her now is her profile; the way her nose turned up right on the very end. Cute as a button! Yes sir, Abigail Vickers was quite a looker!*

Enlarge pattern 115% to measure about 12" wide.

Three Modern Misses

see photo on page 5

Today's woman enjoys a leisurely and independent lifestyle. She is fashionable and active enjoying sailing and...

Enlarge pattern 110% to measure about 14" wide.

Horseback riding. Today's woman is ready to take the reins and show what she can do but she is just as ready to...

Enlarge pattern 120% to measure about 14" wide.

For border: Repeat top design at bottom as shown.

Three Modern Misses
see photo on page 5

Enlarge pattern 110%
to measure about
13" wide.

Take to the road.
Today's woman enjoys
the freedom of being in
the driver's seat.
Once considered bad
taste to be seen
unescorted in public,
women now thrive on
the independence.
It is truly the beginning
of a new era for the
modern woman.

Sheer and Sensational

see photo on page 6

Pattern is
actual size

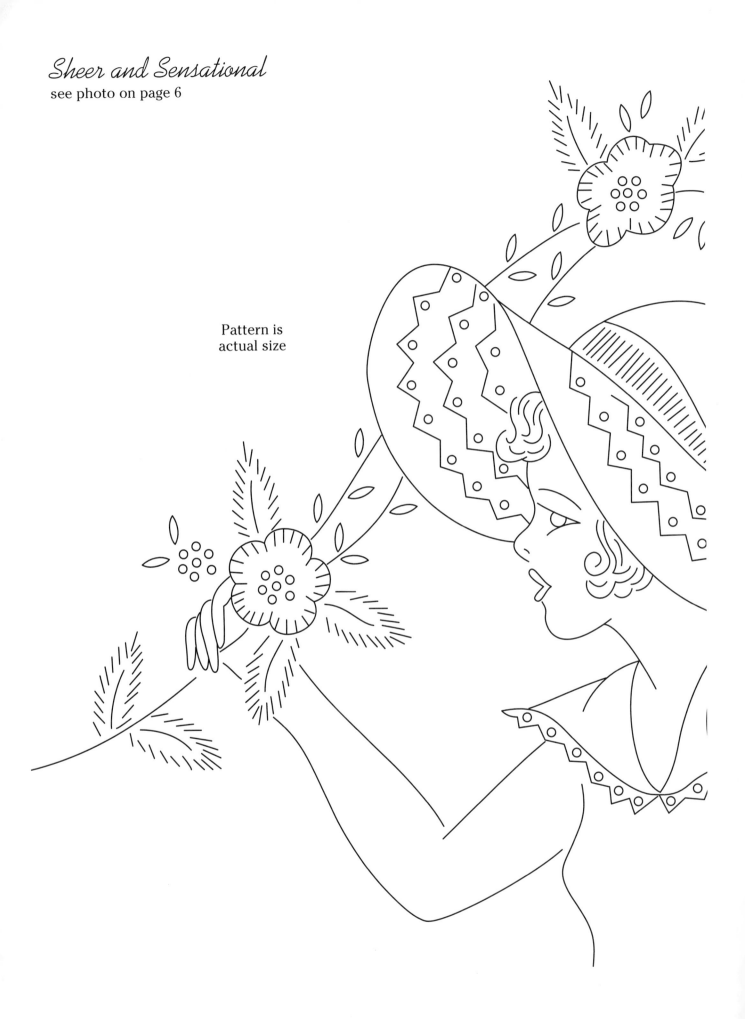

I love to walk among the flowers,
To take in their beautiful shapes and hues,
To smell their sweet perfume.
To receive a precious gift that soothes the soul and gladdens the heart, take a slow walk among the flowers.

Sheer and Sensational
see photo on page 6

Pattern is
actual size

Garden
parties,
teas and
big hats.
Symbols
of a time
gone by.

Sheer and Sensational
see photo on page 7

Pattern is
actual aize

Bottom of Pattern
continues on page 39.

Hat Brim

Pattern
placement
on pillow.

*If beauty is in the eye
of the beholder, then
my eyes, as well as my
heart, are full.*

Center
of
Heart

Heart Top Pillow
Pattern
Copy 1
Trace and
reverse 1 for
other half
of pillow.

Bottom of Pattern
continued from page 38.

Patterns are
actual aize

Pattern is
actual aize

Sheer and
Sensational

Some women love
hats,
With them it's
a passion,
Straw, silk, linen,
organdy or satin,
Dressed up with
stitching, flowers, net
or ribbon,
Worn to the back, to
the front or the side,
A woman's hat is a
prize possession.

A Gracious Gathering

see photo on page 8

Go beyond convention, let your spirit soar.
See the newness in something old,
change the standard. Create!
Find your voice!

Enlarge pattern 110%
to measure about
17" wide.

A Gracious Gathering
see photo on page 8

Enlarge pattern 120%
to measure about
10" wide.

In the afternoon I would sometimes walk to Aunt
Minnie's for afternoon tea. There, the ladies would enjoy
delicious little cakes and share all the latest gossip.
Women can be so terribly wicked!

A Gracious Gathering

see photo on page 8

Enlarge pattern 120%
to measure about
9 " wide.

Dear Meg and I would take strolls in the park dressed in our finest. Linked arm in arm we would take our time, stopping to speak to those we knew and nodding to some we wished we knew. We were so brazen then!

A Gracious Gathering
see photo on page 9

Enlarge pattern 120%
to measure about
12" wide.

I've filled my basket with flowers,
A colorful rainbow of scents.
They will fill my room with happiness
and match my pretty chintz.

Flower design
goes to left of skirt

Enlarge pattern 120%
to measure about
10" wide.

Your beauty is like that of a rose,
Delicious to the eyes, soft and velvety to the touch,
and in possession of an intoxicating scent.

A Gracious Gathering

see photo on page 9

Leisure time calls for fun and games,
Maybe we will do a little dance
or play that patty-cake game.
"Patty-cake, patty-cake, Baker's man,
Make a cake as fast as you can,

Pattern is
actual aize

Pat it, prick it, mark it with a 'T',
put it in the oven for
Tilly and me".

Enlarge pattern 115%
to measure about
9" wide.

CHURCH ON SUNDAY

Sundays are a day of rest,
A day to give thanks,
A day to visit with friends and family,
and of course,
share a good Sunday dinner.

Enlarge pattern 110%
to measure about
7" wide.

Saturdays are reserved for baking.
I kneed the dough for the bread,
Cut up apples and peaches for the pies,
Make up frosting for cakes,
Feed my friend Fido, and then to bed.

Pattern is
actual aize

MARKET ON THURSDAY

To market, to market to buy my goods,
Food for the table, cloth for a dress,
A bonnet, some ribbon and thread.
Market days are really the best!

Enlarge pattern 115%
to measure about
9" wide.

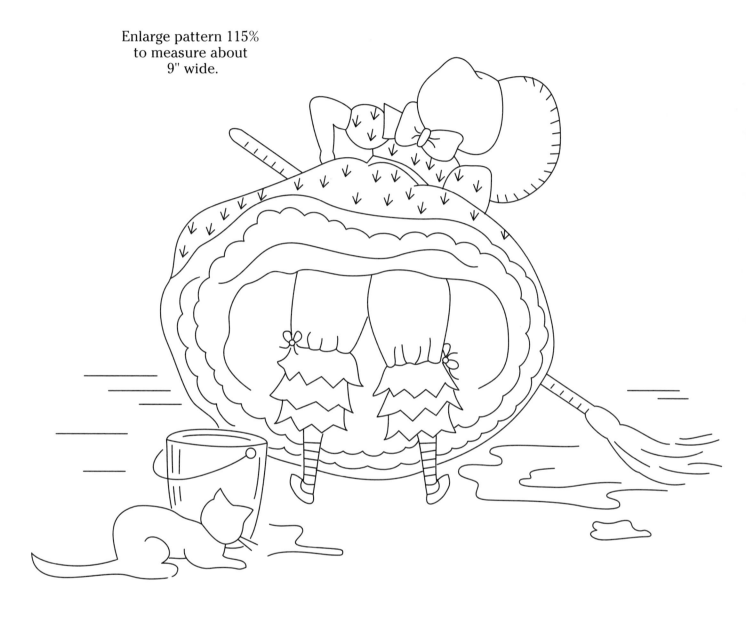

CLEAN ON FRIDAY

Friday brings sweeping and mopping,
And cleaning the house,
Even setting a trap for that little mouse.
Alas, a woman's work is never done.

Patterns are
actual size

Sundays are for church, picking flowers for
the dinner table, eating good food, resting,
socializing and planning the next week.
Sometimes we gather in the parlor and have
happy sing-a-longs or put on plays that the
children have written. Of course I am always
nominated to help with the costumes.
Sundays are still my favorite day of the
week. Did I say it was a day of rest?

Rub-a-dub-
dub the wash
is in the tub.
The blueing
is done, the
starching too,
I'll hang
them on the
line and I'll
be through.

MONDAY

Sprinkle
and iron,
that's what
I do,
One day a
week until I
am through.

TUESDAY

On Wednesdays
I organize my
sewing.
First comes the
mending and
darning,
Next, my new
dress,
Then it's my
sampler, I like
it the best!

WEDNESDAY

Off to the
market on
Thursdays,
I try to
follow my
list,
Until I see a
new bonnet I
just can't
resist.

THURSDAY

Patters are
actual size

"Cleanliness
is next to
Godliness",
my mothers
favorite
saying.
On Fridays
I have both!

FRIDAY

Kitchen duty is
on Saturday.
All the breads,
pastries and
butter are made
for the week.
After that it's
time to clean up
the sink.

SATURDAY

The Simple Things

see photo on page 11

Pattern is
actual size

I'll put on my apron and make my house shine,
I'll cook up the dinner and make it divine.

Pattern is
actual size

Father has a favorite cup
he uses every day,
Mother says he needs a mustache
cup to chase lip mess away.

The Simple Things
see photo on page 11

Pattern is
actual size

Polishing the silver can be a big job,
But I won't stop working 'til I've done the whole lot.

Patterns are
actual size

Congratulations
to the
Mr. and Mrs.
Join us for our
first
anniversary
party.
There will be
parlor games
and
refreshments.

Sheer and Sensational

see photo on page 6

Enlarge pattern 110%
to measure about
14" wide.

Lovely
lady with
eyes of
blue,
I think I'll
ask to
marry you.
If you say
yes, and be
my wife,
I'll be the
proudest
man alive.

Lace Placement

Pattern is
actual size

*A late afternoon walk is good for the figure, but make sure
you have your parasol to keep the sun off your face.
This is most important.*

Dreams of Leisure
see photo on page 12

Ric Rac Stitch Line

Ric Rac Stitch Line

Enlarge pattern 120%
to measure about
11" wide.

Dear Madam,

I hope you will not think me too forward in writing to you. I must tell you that you have been on my mind since our last meeting in your garden. Here, I must say, of all the flowers in the garden, you were the prize. Until we meet again - Your humble servant,

Kitridge DuBerry

Pattern is
actual size

Butterfly, butterfly, where do you call home?
A tree, the grass or prehaps a garden path?

Dreams of Leisure
see photo on page 12

Enlarge pattern 110%
to measure about
14" wide.

Play days
are what
leisure
time is all
about.
Here a
young
woman
sways to
a song in
her head
while
twirling
a ribbon.

In your pretty bonnet,
With all the flowers on it,
You're sure to outshine the others,
at the garden party today!

Enlarge pattern 110%
to measure about
14" wide.

Stitch Braid Here

Dreams of Leisure
see photo on page 12

Off the shoulder gowns, big hats and yards of ribbon and flowers are what make today's fashions so popular. Add a pinch of rouge to the cheeks for a healthy flushed look and you'll have young men's heads turning.

Enlarge pattern 110% to measure about 14" wide.

Dreams of Leisure
see photo on page 12

Enlarge pattern 110%
to measure about
15" wide.

Lovely girl at the garden gate,
Stands and waits for her beau
Is she early or is he late?

Dreams of Leisure
see photo on page 13

Pattern is
actual size

Two twin girls, bashful and shy,
Hide their faces,
As if to cry.

Pattern is
actual size

First a giggle, then a sigh,
Makes it clear that they won't cry,
It's just a suitor riding by.

Dreams of Leisure
see photo on page 13

This pattern makes a lovely pillowcase treatment for a girl's room.
The hat, dress and ruffle at the bottom are in matching fabric. The ruffle creates a dimensional effect along with the embroidered flowers.

Pattern is actual size

Note: When making 2 pillowcases, reverse 1 pattern.

*I'm a potholder girl and
I help out in the kitchen.
I must say I come highly
recommended by the mistress
of the house.*

Pattern is
actual size

Pocket is actual size

Apron Pocket
Cut 2 - Reverse 1

*"Happy birthday
to you,
Happy birthday
to you,
Happy birthday
to you,
Happy birthday
dear Sally,
Happy birthday
to you.
And may you have
many more,"*

Enlarge pattern 130%
to measure about
22" wide.

pattern continued on
pagees 76 - 77

This special apron will be remembered
for years to come by your children
and grandchildren.

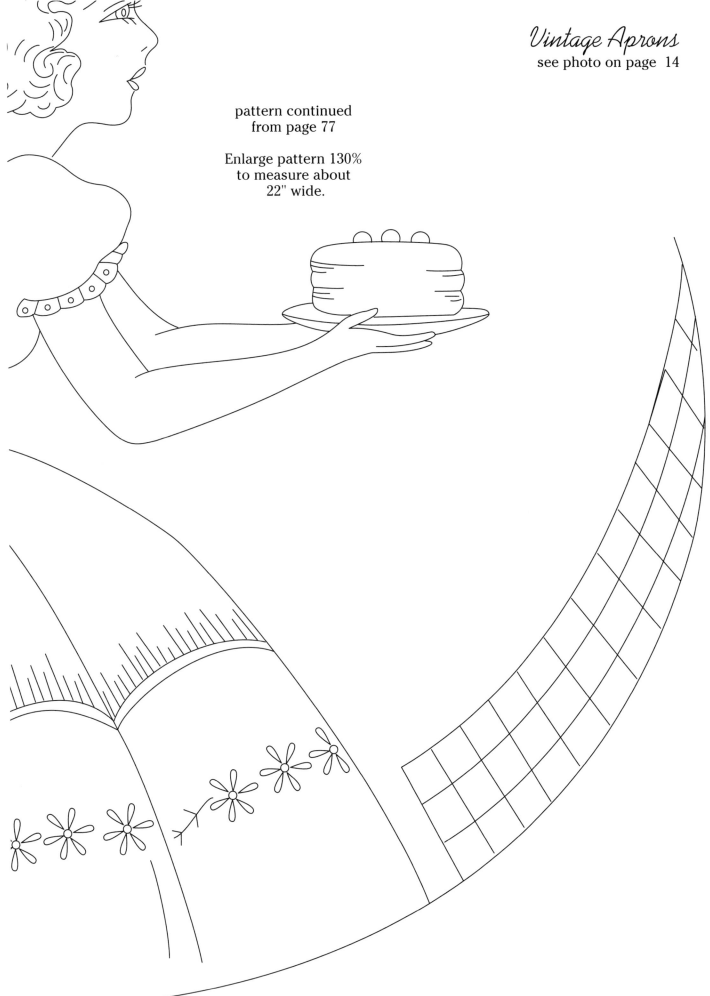

pattern continued
from page 77

Enlarge pattern 130%
to measure about
22" wide.

I have a new
bonnet with bright
ribbons on it.
There are flowers
and stitching
and such.
I'll wear it tomorrow
to go into town,

Enlarge pattern 110%
to measure about
9" wide.

To take tea with my good
friend Lanore.
Other bonnets will be there,
but none will compare with
my bright new
bonnet fare.

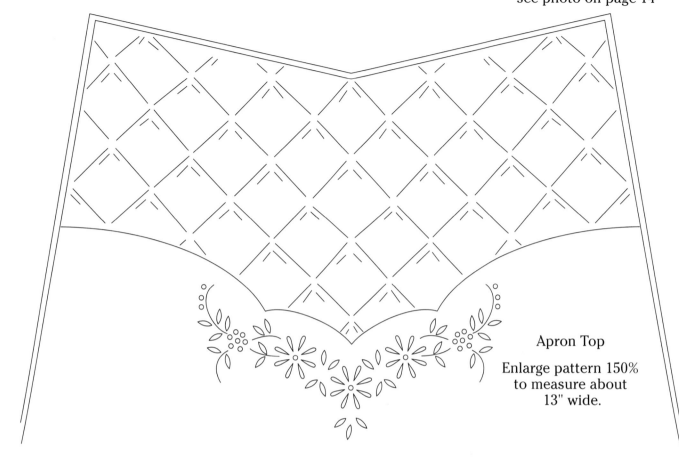

Apron Top

Enlarge pattern 150%
to measure about
13" wide.

*The stitching at the top and
bottom of this design
give this wonderful
apron added punch.*

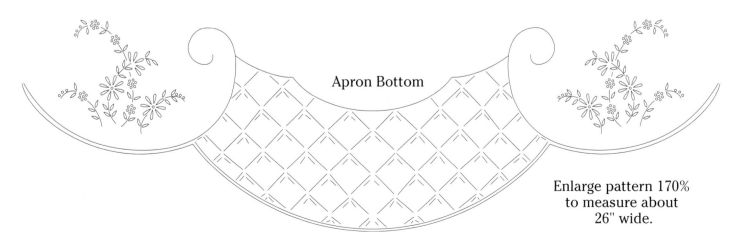

Apron Bottom

Enlarge pattern 170%
to measure about
26" wide.

Vintage Aprons
see photo on page 15

As I walked in
my garden
today, I noticed
a large-winged
butterfly flitting
from flower to
flower.
Then, suddenly,
it fluttered
'round my head
happily as if
thanking me for
the garden.

Enlarge pattern 110%
to measure about
17" wide.

Apron Pocket
Cut 1

Enlarge pattern 110%
to measure about
5" wide.

*Little bird, little bird, if I set you free
Do you promise to return to me?
After you romp and play, will you come
home, will you return to me?*

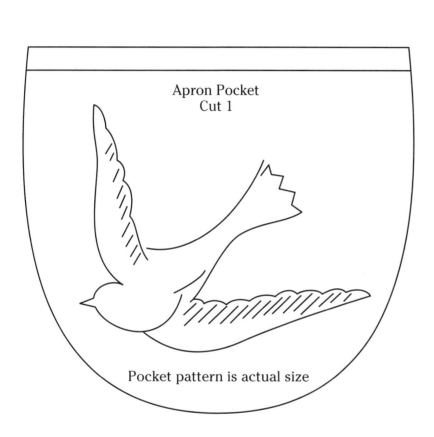

Apron Pocket
Cut 1

Pocket pattern is actual size

Vintage Aprons
see photo on page 15

Enlarge pattern 110%
to measure about
16" wide.

Vintage Aprons
see photo on page 15

What better way to spend your time
than catching butterflies.
Ladies of Leisure are as free as the
butterflies they chase.
However, it is important to remember
that you are a lady.

Pattern is
actual size

Ladies should always maintain proper etiquette, no matter what the sport, and always try to remain graceful.
There are certain gestures and poses that are unattractive, so do watch your posture.
Remember, people may be watching.

Blue Pin Lady

Blue Pin Lady Base
Cut 1 on fold
Blue fabric

FINISHED SIZE: 8" x 3³/4"

MATERIALS:
- Blue porcelain doll top or 7" doll
- 6" x 12¹/2" piece of Blue fabric for base
- 3¹/4" x 12¹/2" piece of White calico
- Two 3" x 37" pieces of Blue netting
- Polyester stuffing
- 3³/4" cardboard circle
- 3" circle of Light Blue felt
- White and Blue sewing threads

Sew across the gathered opening at the bottom.

BASE:
1. Use ¹/4" seam allowance throughout.
2. With right sides facing, sew Blue fabric together across 6" sides to form a tube. Turn tube to the right side.
3. Fold back ¹/4" around the bottom of the tube. Gather end to form a 2" circle. Secure thread, but do not cut it.
4. Insert cardboard circle into the top of the tube. Push the circle to the bottom of the tube, centered over the opening of the gathers at the bottom. Sew back and forth across the opening of the gathers to secure the fabric.
5. Stuff the tube firmly with polyester. Insert doll into center before completing stuffing.
6. Fold back ¹/4" around the top of the tube. Gather top of tube tightly to fit around doll. Secure thread.
7. Glue felt circle to cover gathers at the bottom of the base.

SKIRT:
1. With right sides facing, sew Calico fabric across 6" sides to form a tube. Turn tube to the right side.
2. Fold back ¹/8" twice around the bottom of the tube. Topstitch hem.
3. Fold back ¹/4" around the top of the tube. Place skirt on doll. Gather top of tube tightly to fit around doll. Secure thread but do not cut it. Whip stitch gathered edge of skirt to gathered edge of base.
4. Fold each piece of netting in half lengthwise. Gather folded edge, secure thread but do not cut it. Sew gathers around base 1³/4" above the bottom of the base.
5. Sew running stitches around the skirt ¹/2" above the hem. Gather skirt evenly to fit over the top of the netting. Use small stitches to secure the gathers to the base.

Place on fold

Blue Pin Lady Skirt
Cut 1 on fold
Calico fabric

Place on fold

*All ladies need a pincushion
and here is the answer.
Slip these lovely skirts over
porcelain figurines to add
boudoir glamour to your room.*

**Pink Pin Lady Base
Cut 1 on fold
Pink fabric**

Pink Pin Lady

FINISHED SIZE: 6" x 4"

MATERIALS:
- Pink porcelain doll top or 5" doll
- 6$^1/2$" x 13$^1/2$" piece of Pink fabric for base
- 4$^3/4$" x 28$^1/2$" piece of Light Pink satin
- 3" x 14$^1/2$" piece of White scalloped lace trim
- Polyester stuffing
- 4" cardboard circle
- 3$^1/2$" circle of Pink felt
- Pink sewing thread

BASE:
Assemble the base as for the Blue Pin Lady.

SKIRT:
1. With right sides facing, sew Pink satin fabric across 4$^3/4$" sides to form a tube. Turn tube to the right side.
2. Fold back $^1/4$" around the top of tube. Sew running stitches around top of tube close to the edge. Place skirt on doll. Gather top of tube tightly to fit around doll. Secure thread but do not cut it. Whip stitch gathered edge to gathered edge of base.
3. With right sides facing, sew lace across 3" sides to form a tube. Turn tube to the right side.
4. Sew running stitches around top of tube close to the edge. Place skirt on doll. Gather top of tube tightly to fit around doll. Secure thread but do not cut it. Whip stitch gathered edge to gathered edge of satin skirt. Use small stitches to secure the hem edge of the lace to the base.

Place on fold

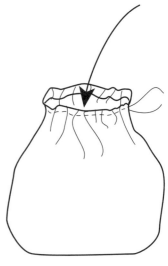

Insert the doll top into the base when it is almost full of stuffing. (If you are using a full doll, put it into the base when it is about half full of stuffing.) Gather the top of the base around the doll.

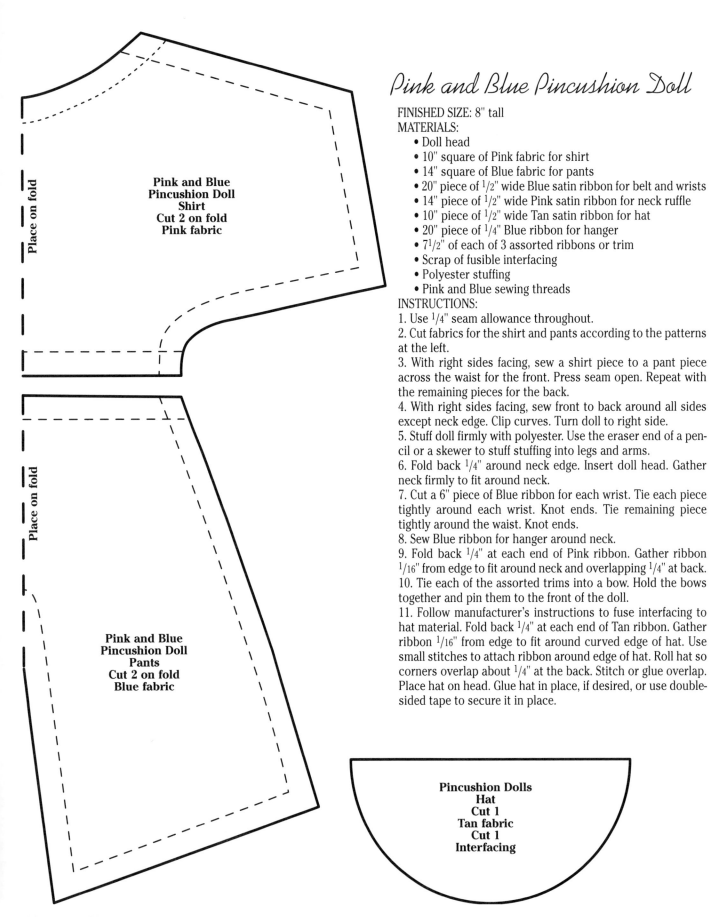

Perky Pincushion Dolls
see photo on page 17

Pink and Blue Pincushion Doll Shirt
Cut 2 on fold
Pink fabric

Place on fold

Pink and Blue Pincushion Doll Pants
Cut 2 on fold
Blue fabric

Place on fold

Pincushion Dolls Hat
Cut 1 Tan fabric
Cut 1 Interfacing

Pink and Blue Pincushion Doll

FINISHED SIZE: 8" tall
MATERIALS:
- Doll head
- 10" square of Pink fabric for shirt
- 14" square of Blue fabric for pants
- 20" piece of $1/2$" wide Blue satin ribbon for belt and wrists
- 14" piece of $1/2$" wide Pink satin ribbon for neck ruffle
- 10" piece of $1/2$" wide Tan satin ribbon for hat
- 20" piece of $1/4$" Blue ribbon for hanger
- $7^1/2$" of each of 3 assorted ribbons or trim
- Scrap of fusible interfacing
- Polyester stuffing
- Pink and Blue sewing threads

INSTRUCTIONS:
1. Use $1/4$" seam allowance throughout.
2. Cut fabrics for the shirt and pants according to the patterns at the left.
3. With right sides facing, sew a shirt piece to a pant piece across the waist for the front. Press seam open. Repeat with the remaining pieces for the back.
4. With right sides facing, sew front to back around all sides except neck edge. Clip curves. Turn doll to right side.
5. Stuff doll firmly with polyester. Use the eraser end of a pencil or a skewer to stuff stuffing into legs and arms.
6. Fold back $1/4$" around neck edge. Insert doll head. Gather neck firmly to fit around neck.
7. Cut a 6" piece of Blue ribbon for each wrist. Tie each piece tightly around each wrist. Knot ends. Tie remaining piece tightly around the waist. Knot ends.
8. Sew Blue ribbon for hanger around neck.
9. Fold back $1/4$" at each end of Pink ribbon. Gather ribbon $1/16$" from edge to fit around neck and overlapping $1/4$" at back.
10. Tie each of the assorted trims into a bow. Hold the bows together and pin them to the front of the doll.
11. Follow manufacturer's instructions to fuse interfacing to hat material. Fold back $1/4$" at each end of Tan ribbon. Gather ribbon $1/16$" from edge to fit around curved edge of hat. Use small stitches to attach ribbon around edge of hat. Roll hat so corners overlap about $1/4$" at the back. Stitch or glue overlap. Place hat on head. Glue hat in place, if desired, or use double-sided tape to secure it in place.

Blue & Coral Pincushion Dolls

FINISHED SIZE: 9" tall

MATERIALS FOR EACH DOLL:
- Doll head
- Two 9" squares of Blue or Coral fabric for body
- 4" square of Tan fabric for hat
- 9" piece of $3/4$" wide complementary color satin ribbon for belt
- 16" piece of $1/2$" wide complementary color satin ribbon for neck ruffle
- 10" piece of $1/2$" wide Tan satin ribbon for hat
- 20" piece of Blue ribbon for hanger
- $7^1/2$" of each of 3 assorted ribbons or trim
- Scrap of fusible interfacing
- Polyester stuffing
- Blue or Coral sewing threads

INSTRUCTIONS:

1. Use $1/4$" seam allowance throughout.

2. Cut fabric for the body according to the pattern at the right.

3. With right sides facing, sew front to back around all sides except neck edge. Clip curves. Turn doll to right side.

4. Stuff doll firmly with polyester. Use the eraser end of a pencil or a skewer to stuff stuffing into legs and arms.

5. Fold back $1/4$" around neck edge. Insert doll head. Gather neck firmly to fit around neck.

6. Tie the 9" piece of ribbon around the waist. Knot ends. Sew Blue ribbon for hanger around neck.

7. Fold back $1/4$" at each end of neck ruffle ribbon. Gather ribbon $1/16$" from edge to fit from front center of waist, around back of neck and overlapping first end at front. Pin or stitch ruffle in place.

8. Follow manufacturer's instructions to fuse interfacing to hat material. Fold back $1/4$" at each end of Tan ribbon. Gather ribbon $1/16$" from edge to fit around curved edge of hat. Use small stitches to attach ribbon around edge of hat. Roll hat so corners overlap about $1/4$" at the back. Stitch or glue overlap. Place hat on head. Glue hat in place, if desired, or use double-sided tape to secure it in place.

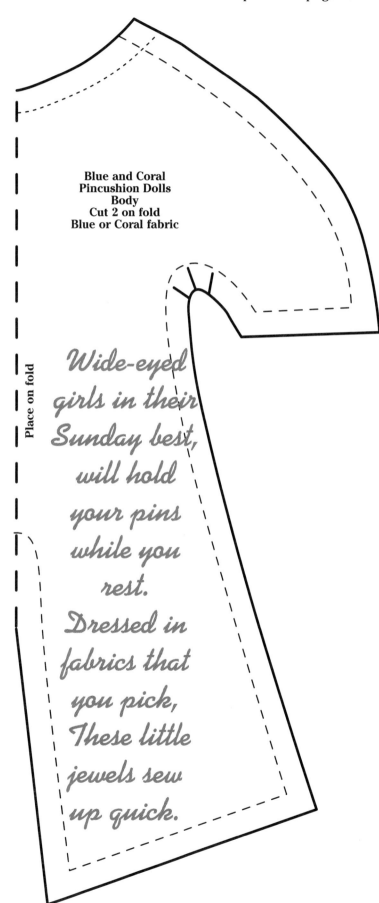

Blue and Coral Pincushion Dolls Body Cut 2 on fold Blue or Coral fabric

Place on fold

Wide-eyed girls in their Sunday best, will hold your pins while you rest. Dressed in fabrics that you pick, These little jewels sew up quick.

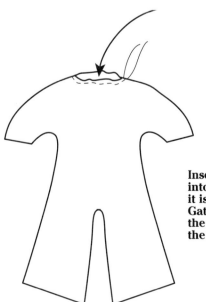

Insert the doll head into the body when it is fully stuffed. Gather the top of the body around the doll's neck.

Exotic Ladies
see photo on page 16

Center Stage
Light up
your next
project with
this
glamorous
creature.

Skirt
Placement

Pattern is
actual size

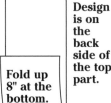

Exotic Lady Bag

FINISHED SIZE: 8" x 8"

MATERIALS:
- 17" x 24¹/₂" piece of Peach silk or polished cotton
- 6¹/₂" x 4¹/₂" piece of Black tulle
- 28" piece of ³/₈" wide complementary trim
- 8¹/₂" x 24¹/₂" piece of batting
- Black and Orange fabric paints
- Fine tip brush and No. 3 round tip brush
- 2 velcro circle sets or 2 snap sets
- 1 skein of DMC embroidery floss 351 Coral
- Peach and Black sewing threads

DESIGN:

1. Cut two 8¹/₂" x 24¹/₂" pieces of silk or satin.
2. Transfer the design for the lady, above, onto the center of the bottom third of one piece. The bottom edge of the skirt should be 1" from the edge of the fabric.
3. With Orange paint and fine tip brush, paint dress bodice with squiggles of Orange, dot lips and paint top of hair comb.
4. With Orange paint and larger brush, paint feathers on fan.
5. With Black paint and fine tip brush, paint hair, eyes, lines for hair comb and fan, and straps and sides of dress.
6. Use 2 strands of floss to embroider side of face, neck and arms.

PURSE:

1. Use ¹/₄" seam allowance throughout.
2. Lay the fabric pieces with the design right sides together on surface. Place batting on top. Sew pieces together through all layers, leaving a 4" opening along one side.
3. Trim batting close to seam.
4. Turn the pieces so the design and plain fabric enclose the batting.
5. Lay design side down, with the design at the top. Fold up 8" from the bottom. Hand sew or topstitch to close the sides.
6. Sew Velcro circles or snap sets to the top corners and to the bottom corners above the fold.
7. Gather the top of the tulle to fill the waistline. Sew in place. Gather skirt above hem. Cut a 2¹/₂" piece of trim. Fold back ¹/₄" at either end over edge of tulle. Sew skirt and trim in place.
8. Fold back ¹/₄" at either end of remaining trim. Sew remaining trim around outer edges of design area, overlapping ends ¹/₂" over top.

Design is on the back side of the top part.

Fold up 8" at the bottom.

Ladies on Parade
see photo on page 99

Five different
motifs make up our
Ladies on Parade
Quilt.
Some hold flowers
and others parasols
or paddles.

Enlarge pattern 110%
to measure about
12" wide.

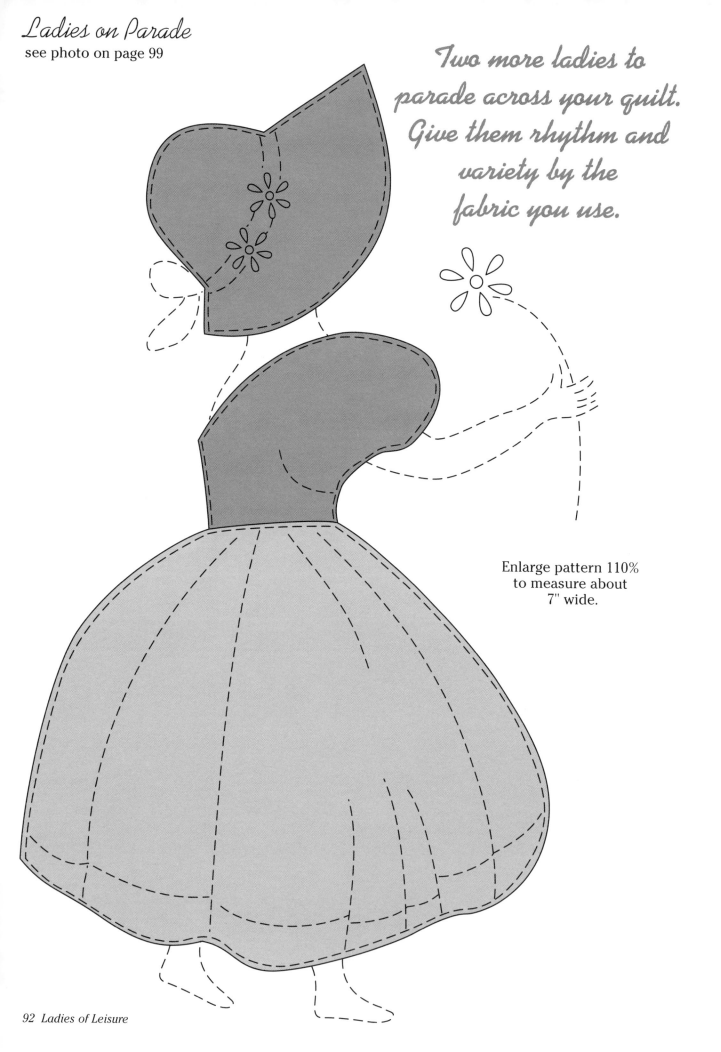

Two more ladies to
parade across your quilt.
Give them rhythm and
variety by the
fabric you use.

Enlarge pattern 110%
to measure about
7" wide.

Ladies on Parade
see photo on page 99

Enlarge pattern 115%
to measure a little
more than 9" wide.

Ladies on Parade
see photo on
page 99

Enlarge pattern 110%
to measure about
9" wide.

Enlarge pattern 110%
to measure about
7" wide.

Boating Anyone?
A favorite activity
of leisure is boating.
Let's hope this
young girl hands
the paddle to her
beau.

Care of Linens

Washing -

• Test for colorfastness on the seam allowance. Let several drops of water fall through the fabric onto white blotter paper. If color appears, the fabric is not colorfast.

• To set dye, soak fabric in water and vinegar.

• Wash with a very mild detergent or soap, using tepid water. Follow all label instructions carefully.

• Do not use chlorine bleach on fine linen. Whiten it by hanging it in full sunlight.

Stain Removal -

• Grease - Use a presoak fabric treatment and wash in cold water.

• Nongreasy - Soak in cold water to neutralize the stain. Apply a presoak and then wash in cold water.

• Ballpoint Ink - Place on an absorbent material and soak with denatured or rubbing alcohol. Apply room temperature glycerin and flush with water. Finally, apply ammonia and quickly flush with water.

• Candle Wax - Place fabric between layers of absorbent paper and iron on low setting. Change paper as it absorbs wax. If a stain remains, wash with peroxide bleach.

• Rust - Remove with lemon juice, oxalic acid or hydrofluoric acid.

Storage -

• Wash and rinse thoroughly in soft water.

• Do not size or starch.

• Place cleaned linen on acid-free tissue paper and roll loosely.

• Line storage boxes with a layer of acid-free tissue paper.

• Place rolled linens in a box. Do not stack. Weight causes creases.

• Do not store linens in plastic bags.

• Hang linen clothing in a muslin bag or cover with a cotton sheet.

'Tinting' with Crayons

Crayons Aren't Paints - Even though ironing softens the crayon, their hard nature means that some of the texture of the fabric and the strokes you make will show through - just like when you make a rubbing over a penny. Making your strokes in the same direction can be challenging in large areas, which is why projects with smaller individual areas of color are best suited to crayon tinting.

Tip: Practice on extra muslin first.

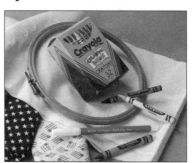

Supplies - Muslin fabric, 24 colors of crayons (or more), embroidery floss, embroidery hoop, micron pen, needle

Crayon Hints - Besides being convenient, crayons come in beautiful colors and aren't intimidating. Simply color in the spaces to create the look you want.

Build Up Color, Edges In

Add layers of crayon color with the strokes going in one direction, or opposite directions for a darker effect. Start lightly - you can always add more. Shading built up from the edges inward helps model or add depth to pieces, so that the tinted areas are not only colorful but three-dimensional as well. You can even choose to leave an area completely open to give a strong highlight.

Use the Correct End

For filling in color, the blunt end of the crayon works best and it works even better if its hard edge is rounded off a little before you start. Keep the pointed end for details or adding a fine shaded line to edges.

Tip: Let the Fabric Do the Work

A shaded fabric (white on white or off white) adds depth to your shading. Larger designs are a little better than fine ones because they give more variety.

1. Position fabric over a pattern, secure corners with masking tape.

Trace pattern outline directly onto muslin with a blue-line water erase pen or a pencil.

2. Place fabric on a pad of extra fabric and color areas with regular children's crayons.

Color the pattern well with crayon color.

3. Sandwich the fabric between two sheets of plain paper.

Iron on 'cotton' setting to 'set' the crayon colors.

4. If desired, back design with another piece of fabric, place fabric or layers in an embroidery hoop.

Use 3-ply floss to outline the design.

Embroidery Stitches

Working with Floss. Separate embroidery floss.

Use 24" lengths of floss and a #8 embroidery needle.

Use 2 to 3 ply floss to outline large elements of the design and to embroider larger and more stylized patterns.

Use 2 ply for the small details on some items.

Pay attention to backgrounds.

When working with lighter-colored fabrics, do not carry dark flosses across large unworked background areas. Stop and start again to prevent unsightly 'ghost strings' from showing through the front.

Another option is to back tinted muslin with another layer of muslin before you add embroidery stitches. This will help keep 'ghost strings' from showing.

Blanket Stitch

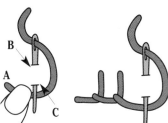

Come up at A, hold the thread down with your thumb, go down at B. Come back up at C with the needle tip over the thread. Pull the stitch into place. Repeat, outlining with the bottom legs of the stitch. Use this stitch to edge fabrics.

Chain Stitch

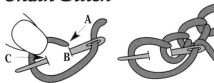

Come up at A. To form a loop, hold the thread down with your thumb, go down at B (as close as possible to A). Come back up at C with the needle tip over the thread. Repeat to form a chain.

Cross Stitch

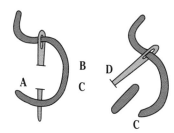

Make a diagonal Straight stitch (up at A, down at B) from upper right to lower left. Come up at C and go down at D to make another diagonal Straight stitch the same length as the first one. The stitch will form an X.

French Knot

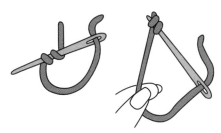

Come up at A. Wrap the floss around the needle 2 to 3 times. Insert the needle close to A. Hold the floss and pull the needle through the loops gently.

Herringbone Stitch

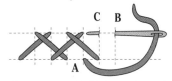 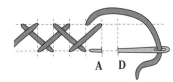

Come up at A. Make a slanted stitch to the top right, inserting the needle at B. Come up a short distance away at C.

Insert the needle at D to complete the stitch. Bring the needle back up at the next A to begin a new stitch. Repeat.

Lazy Daisy Stitch

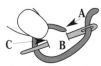

Come up at A. Go down at B (right next to A) to form a loop. Come back up at C with the needle tip over the thread. Go down at D to make a small anchor stitch over the top of the loop.

Running Stitch

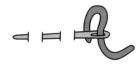

Come up at A. Weave the needle through the fabric, making short, even stitches. Use this stitch to gather fabrics, too.

Satin Stitch

Work small straight stitches close together and at the same angle to fill an area with stitches. Vary the length of the stitches as required to keep the outline of the area smooth.

Stem Stitch

Work from left to right to make regular, slanting stitches along the stitch line. Bring the needle up above the center of the last stitch. Also called 'Outline' stitch.

Straight Stitch

Come up at A and go down at B to form a simple flat stitch. Use this stitch for hair for animals and for simple petals on small flowers.

Whip Stitch

Insert the needle under a few fibers of one layer of fabric. Bring the needle up through the other layer of fabric. Use this stitch to attach the folded raw edges of fabric to the back of pieces or to attach bindings around the edges of quilts and coverlets.

Ladies on Parade Quilt

FINISHED SIZE: 76" x 76"

MATERIALS:
- 44" wide, 100% cotton fabrics:
    - A - 3$^1/4$ yards White fabric for design blocks
    - B - 7$^1/2$ yards Bright Pink fabric for sashing strips, borders, backing and binding
    - C - 12" squares of each of 25 assorted print fabrics for appliques
    - D - 12" squares of each of 25 assorted solid fabrics to complement the print fabrics for appliques
    - E - $^1/8$ yard of Medium Green for sashing and corner squares
- 80" x 80" piece of batting
- 5 skeins of DMC embroidery floss 310 Black, 2 skeins 913 Medium Green and 1 skein of each of 25 assorted colors to complement the print applique fabrics
- Pink sewing thread

DESIGN BLOCKS:

1. Cut twenty-five 12$^1/2$" x 12$^1/2$" squares from A.

2. Transfer one of each of the designs on pages 91 - 95 onto the center of each of 5 A squares. Each block on each row will have the same design. Each row is a different design.

3. Make a template for the pieces of each design on pages 91 - 95. Refer to the photo to determine whether a piece is to be cut from a print or solid fabric. If desired, use a glue stick to attach the templates for the print pieces to the wrong side of the C squares. Place the right side of the template down.

4. Repeat to attach the templates for the solid pieces to the back of the appropriate D squares.

5. Cut around each template, leaving a $^1/4$" seam allowance around all edges. Clip curves.

6. Place each piece right side down on an ironing board. Spray the edges of each piece with heavy-duty spray starch. Fold back the $^1/4$" seam allowance around the edges and iron it in place. Ease curves, make corners crisp.

7. Applique the pieces in place.

8. Use 2 strands of Green floss to embroider running stitch stems and lazy daisy leaves.

9. Use 2 strands of Black floss to embroider running stitches along the remaining dashed lines on each design.

10. Use 2 strands of the assorted complementary flosses to embroider the flowers.

SASHING:

1. Use $^1/4$" seam allowance throughout.

2. Cut forty 3" x 12$^1/2$" strips from B.

3. With right sides facing, sew a row of same design applique blocks alternately with four 12$^1/2$" strips.

4. Repeat with the remaining same design blocks and four 12$^1/2$" strips to make a total of five 5-block rows. Lay rows aside.

Sew 5 rows with 5 design blocks and 4 sashing strips.

5. Cut sixteen 3" x 3" squares from E.

6. With right sides facing, sew four rows of five 12$^1/2$" strips alternately with four 3" squares.

Sew 5 rows with 5 design blocks and 4 sashing strips.

7. Sew the five design rows alternately with the four strips and squares rows. Trim edges even.

BORDERS:

1. Cut 2 side borders each 3$^1/2$" x 70$^1/2$" from B.

2. Cut 2 top and bottom borders 3$^1/2$" x 70$^1/2$" from B.

3. Cut 4 corner squares 3$^1/2$" x 3$^1/2$" from E.

4. With right sides facing, sew the side borders in place. Trim all ends even.

5. With right sides facing, sew a 3$^1/2$" square to each end of each top and bottom border. Sew the top and bottom borders in place. Trim all edges even.

BACKING:

1. Cut two 40$^1/2$" x 80" pieces from A. With right sides facing, sew the pieces together along one long edge. Press the seam open.

2. Layer the backing, batting and the assembled top to form a sandwich. Center the quilt top on the batting. Baste all of the layers together.

3. Quilt the quilt as desired.

4. Remove the basting stitches. Trim the batting even with the edges of the quilt top.

BINDING:

1. Cut 2$^1/2$" strips from B for the binding.

2. Refer to the instructions on page 19 to attach the binding.

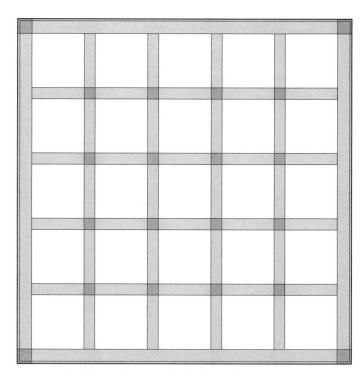

Ladies on Parade Quilt Assembly Diagram

MANY THANKS to my friends for their cheerful help and wonderful ideas!
Kathy McMillan • Jennifer Laughlin • Patty Williams • Marti Wyble
Charlie Davis Young • Margaret Allyson
David & Donna Thomason